ENFJ: Understanding & Relating with the Teacher

MBTI Personality Types Series

By: Clayton Geoffreys

Table of Contents

Foreword

Have you ever been curious about why you behave certain ways? Well I know I have always pondered this question. When I first learned about psychology in high school, I immediately was hooked. Learning about the inner workings of the human mind fascinated me. Human beings are some of the most impressive species to ever walk on this earth. Over the years, one thing I've learned from my life experiences is that having a high degree of self-awareness is critical to get to where you want to go in life and to achieve what you want to accomplish. A person who is not self-aware is a person who lives life blindly, accepting what some label as fate. I began intensely studying psychology to better understand myself, and through my journey, I discovered the Myers Brigg Type Indicator (MBTI), a popular personality test that distinguishes between sixteen types of individuals. I hope to cover some of the most prevalent personality types of the MBTI test and share my findings with you through a series of books. Rather than just reading this for the sake of reading it though, I want you to reflect on the information that will be shared with you. Hopefully from reading *ENFJ: Understanding & Relating with the Teacher*, I can pass along some of the abundance of information I have learned about ENFJs in general, how they view the world, as well as their greatest strengths and weaknesses. Thank you for purchasing my book. Hope you enjoy and if you do, please do not forget to leave a review! Also, check out my website at claytongeoffreys.com to join my exclusive list where I let you know about my latest books. To thank you for your purchase, you can go to my site to download a free copy of *33 Life Lessons: Success Principles, Career Advice & Habits of Successful People*. In the book, you'll learn from some of the greatest thought leaders of different industries on what it takes to become successful and how to live a great life.

Cheers,

Clayton Geoffreys

An Introduction to MBTI

The world we live in is filled with unique and diverse individuals. In fact, we often struggle with trying to understand what makes other people tick. Even self-awareness can be elusive at times. Fortunately, there are tools to help us identify someone's natural tendencies and inclinations, including our own.

The Myers-Briggs Type Indicator (MBTI) assessment is one example. It is an effective method of gauging someone's personality type based on their answers to a series of questions designed to assess how they gather information, make decisions, and perceive the world. The MBTI operates on the basis that everything you do is a reflection of your personality. Even your seemingly erratic behaviors are rooted in the natural framework of who you are.

Published in 1962 by Katharine Cook Briggs and Isabel Briggs-Myers, the test was originally devised to help women choose jobs. The mother-daughter team was inspired by the theories of Carl Jung who speculated that there are four primary functions by which people make choices and perceive the world. They studied Jung's theories in depth, adding their own research and ideas to create what has now become one of the oldest and most popular personality evaluations in existence.

Do you like being surrounded by other people? Do you prefer spending time alone? Are you comfortable with chaos? These are just some of the questions the MBTI assessment asks in order to actuate your personality type. The questions are specifically designed to target four dimensions of an individual's psyche. Each dimension consists of two contrasting functions: extroversion vs. introversion, sensing vs. intuition, thinking vs. feeling, and perceiving vs. judging. Although it is possible for a person to possess both qualities, the test determines which function is more dominant. For example, you may display both introverted and extroverted behaviors, but introversion is your more dominant function.

Your results are combined to form a four-letter acronym that represents your personality type. There are sixteen possible combinations. The resulting types are then grouped according to temperament. ISFJ, ISTJ, ESFJ, and ESTJ are classified as Guardians. ESFP, ESTP, ISFP, and ISTP are classified as Artisans. ENTP, ENTJ, INTJ, and INTP comprise the Rational group. Finally, ENFJ, INFP, INFJ, and ENFP are classified as Idealists.

The Four Dimensions of the MBTI

You may have noticed that some people can detach themselves from a situation before making a decision, while others lead with their emotions. You may have wondered why some people prefer solitary activities, while others would rather be out with their friends. It all boils down to how they scored in each dimension of the MBTI test.

The MBTI theorizes that your personality can be broken down into four key dimensions. Each dimension represents a different function of your psyche. The results of each dimension are combined to form a four-letter acronym, which refers to your personality type.

The four dimensions are:

1. Extroversion (E) vs. Introversion (I)

The first dimension revolves around energy. Extroverts

are energized when surrounded by other people. If you are an extrovert, you thrive on the stimulus you get from social interactions. You are most comfortable in large crowds and enjoy being the center of attention. Introverts, on the other hand, find extended social interactions draining. If introversion is your dominant attitude, you value privacy and solitude. It is not that you do not like being around other people, it is just that you need moments of quiet reflection to recharge.

2. Intuition (N) vs. Sensing (S)

This dimension refers to the method by which you gather information. If your dominant function is intuition, you are most likely an abstract thinker. You trust your gut and can read between the lines. You believe in first impressions and are focused on the future. Seeing the bigger picture comes naturally to you. When you look at a set of trees, you immediately think "forest." If you lean toward sensing, it means you only trust what you can currently process with your five senses. You need facts. You are a practical thinker who values the here and now. This makes you more realistic and logical.

3. Thinking (T) vs. Feeling (F)

The third dimension relates to your decision-making process. Thinkers, as the name indicates, lead with their heads. If you identify as a thinker, you have the ability to distance yourself from a situation before making a decision. This allows you to make objective choices. Logic and reason are of utmost importance to you. If you are a feeler, you tend to follow your heart. When it comes to making decisions, you are swayed by your emotions. Your choices are generally based on values and principles. This makes you sensitive to other people's feelings, but it also makes you more prone to getting hurt.

4. Judging (J) vs. Perceiving (P)

The fourth dimension gauges the way you regard the

world. If you score higher on the judging scale, it means you value organization and structure. Chances are you adhere to a strict schedule. This makes you responsible and reliable. On the other hand, being inclined toward perception means you are flexible and laid back. You can operate without a pre-existing set of guidelines. In fact, you prefer going with the flow.

Why is the Myers-Briggs Type Indicator Significant?

In this day and time, self-actualization has become a major goal for most people. With that said, an individual's fullest potential cannot be reached without self-awareness. Knowing your personality type will help you assess your natural strengths and weakness, which will then enable you to nurture and overcome them. It can also help you gauge which career paths you are most likely to enjoy and excel in. Furthermore, understanding your personal motivations can provide you with the self-awareness you need to identify potential opportunities for success.

The MBTI test provides useful insight into other people's minds as well. By understanding what makes other people tick, you can build more harmonious interpersonal relationships. It can help you figure out why people behave a certain way during particular situations. When it comes to friendships and romantic relationships, it promotes more open lines of communication, as well as a greater comprehension of their personality framework. Does your significant other get upset when their plans are not followed? Do they walk away during confrontations? Are some of your friends extremely sensitive to criticism? All these questions can be explained by understanding their personality types.

The MBTI test also has numerous practical applications in the workplace and at school. Do you prefer working together with a group or on your own? Do you find it hard to focus on one specific task at a time? Do you prefer certain activities more than others? These are a few things that are linked to your personality. Knowing your type will allow you to adjust your study habits according to what works best for your personality. You can also choose career paths that will most likely give you the satisfaction you require.

In a nutshell, MBTI has become an essential tool in achieving success, be it in the workplace, at home, or in your personal relationships.

Uncovering the "Teachers": Who is an ENFJ?

ENFJ is one of the sixteen personality types based on the MBTI. ENFJs are one of the rare personality types, making up only roughly 2% of the general population. The acronym stands for Extroverted Intuition Feeling Judging.

The cognitive functions of ENFJs are as follows:

- Dominant: Extroverted Feeling (Fe) - Your dominant cognitive function refers to the role you are most comfortable fulfilling. As an ENFJ, your dominant function is Extroverted Feeling. This refers to your desire to build connections with other people which you manifest by reaching out and helping others. You aim to create harmonious interpersonal relationships and are naturally in tune to the emotions of the people around you.

- Auxiliary: Introverted Intuition (Ni) - Your auxiliary function is an extension of your dominant one. In your case, the auxiliary function is Introverted Intuition. This relates to your ability to see the larger picture and assess future possibilities based on your instincts and gut feelings.

- Tertiary: Extroverted Sensing (Se) - The tertiary cognitive function is less developed than the dominant and auxiliary ones; however, there is a high likelihood that this function will become more pronounced later on in your life. As an ENFJ, your tertiary function is Extroverted Sensing. This means that you might eventually start assessing your surroundings based on what you can ascertain with your five physical senses.

- Inferior: Introverted Thinking (Ti) - The inferior function is also known as your Achilles' heel. This means it is the function you are least comfortable with. In ENFJs, the inferior function is Introverted Thinking, which is the direct opposite of the dominant function. Ti requires precision. It focuses on sheer logic rather than values and emotions.

ENFJs, more than any other personality type, are natural born leaders. As an ENFJ, you are passionate and charismatic. People are inexplicably drawn to your strong personality. As such, you are able to influence and motivate others while bringing out the best in them. Your main focus in life is to support and encourage others. Whether it is leading a country toward prosperity or helping in a friend's success, you are equally passionate about the people and causes you believe in.

As an extrovert, you are very charming and outgoing. Your intuition enables you to get a feel for what other people are feeling, even if they do not say it outright. It also gives you the ability to form connections between seemingly unrelated situations. Your inclination toward feeling keeps you compassionate and warm. Your judging allows you to do all this against a backdrop of meticulous planning.

ENFJs are also known as Teachers. Teachers are part of a larger group of personalities called Idealists. While all Idealists have the ability to call forth the potential of people, no other type does it as well as ENFJs. You possess an almost magical gift, which allows you to ignite sparks in other people's imaginations. Your extroversion enables you to reach out to others with ease. Your intuition allows you to tailor your approach depending on who you are with. When these two qualities are combined, you are able to touch other people's lives in an inimitable way. The belief you have in other people is genuine. You believe in their potential, and you trust that they will be able to live up to their fullest potential.

Since you are driven by helping others succeed, you tend to make decisions based on their needs instead of your own. This can cause you to develop a chameleon-like way of interacting; mirroring another person's communication style to relate to them better, which then makes people feel immediately at ease around you.

Among all the personality types, ENFJs are the most people-oriented. You have excellent people skills. You can get almost anyone to do what you want, and you used this to motivate and inspire. However, less-developed ENFJs can sometimes use this ability to manipulate other people.

True to your extroverted nature, you sometimes struggle during moments of solitude. Being alone can cause you to over-analyze every aspect of your life, looking for flaws and shortcomings. As a result, most ENFJs actively avoid being alone.

Why are ENFJs Indispensable Leaders?

No other personality type is more suited for leadership than ENFJs. As an ENFJ, you naturally fare well in positions that allow you to deal with other people. Your charismatic personality and natural ease with words also make you a highly effective leader. It can even be said that leadership is an ENFJ's true calling. It is also important to note that when an ENFJ climbs up the ranks of organizational hierarchy, the goals are not money and power. In fact, you believe that the organization's main purpose is to serve other people.

As a leader, your extroversion allows you to focus on the needs of others. Your intuition enables you to encourage and inspire. Your feeling nature makes you sensitive toward the concerns of your team members. Your judging provides the structure to keep everything organized and pushing forward.

ENFJs are ambitious. Not in a selfish way, mind you,

but in a way that makes you feel like it is your personal responsibility to improve the world and other people's lives. In fact, you tend to measure your own personal success by your ability to enrich others. Because you possess a natural urge to support and encourage, being a leader comes easily to you. Oftentimes, you do not even have to ask for the role. People just automatically look to you for advice, counsel, and guidance. You also have the language skills required to get your message across. In fact, ENFJs are often outstanding public speakers and are known to be smooth-talking persuasion experts. Furthermore, your ability to deal with a diverse range of people enables you to reach out to anyone.

As an ENFJ, your leadership style can be described as enthusiastic and encouraging. You are the type of leader who wants to see their team excel, both as a group and individually. When a member of your team accomplishes something, it makes you feel extremely proud. You are always pushing your team to do their best, and your genuine confidence in their capabilities is often the catalyst they need to realize their full potential. In the workplace, ENFJ leaders are sensitive and communicative. Not only do you strive to get your projects done, you want them to be accomplished in a way that makes all members of your team feel valued and satisfied. This makes you quite popular and well-liked.

Furthermore, you are personally invested in the well-being and success of the people you handle. Whenever a crisis happens, your first thought is about how it will affect the members of your team. You are also sincerely concerned with their personal problems and issues. Sometimes, though, you have the tendency to become too invested. When this happens, you might consider it a personal failure when someone you have invested in falls short of your expectations. You also tend to feel drained when you find yourself surrounded by negative energy.

Due to your inclination toward judging, having multiple things on your plate does not overwhelm you the way it would other personality types. You are able to effectively manage your time while keeping commitments and meeting deadlines. However, your need for structure can sometimes be overshadowed by your need to help other people.

The 7 Greatest Strengths of an ENFJ

As an ENFJ, you possess a number of remarkable strengths that are unique to your personality type. Being aware of your natural gifts and abilities can be the first step toward greater success and personal development. Allow these strengths to flourish.

1. Excellent Verbal Communications Skills

As an ENFJ, you have a natural flair with words. In fact, most ENFJs are excellent public speakers. You are very eloquent and can articulate your thoughts and emotions quite well. When you speak, people automatically listen. This quality is a valued strength, both in the workplace and in personal situations. When combined with your extroverted roots, this enables you to captivate your audience with your words. Furthermore, because you are able to voice your opinions so effectively, communication rarely becomes a problem in your relationships.

2. People Skills and Charm

You are naturally charming, and people cannot help but be drawn to you. You have a sixth sense when it comes to dealing with people, and you instinctively know how to change your overall tone, depending on who you are talking to. Your sensitivity to other people's feelings also helps you evaluate their needs and identify which approach will work best with them. Like a chameleon, you are able to imitate other people's communication styles to better relate to them. Thus, people feel comfortable and at ease around you, even if you have not known them for very long. This is one of the qualities that make you so popular. Your people skills also encourage other people to express themselves and open up.

3. Natural Leadership Skills

No other personality type can handle positions of leadership with more ease than ENFJs. Even when you do not seek out leadership, it naturally falls into your lap. People look up to you and are drawn to the strength of your personality. Your leadership style is driven by your altruistic nature. Helping people and improving the community or organization are your main goals whenever you find yourself in a position of authority. As a leader, you can be described as supportive and encouraging. You believe in a positive and uplifting approach as opposed to one that is overbearing and domineering.

4. Responsible and Reliable

Due to your inclination toward judging, you work best against a backdrop of structure and organization. You honor your commitments and fulfill your responsibilities. When you take on a task, you make it your personal duty to ensure that it is seen to completion. In fact, it is almost impossible for you to leave a project unfinished or incomplete. Not only does this speak to your need for closure, but also the loyalty you have to the people and causes you care about.

5. Loyalty

As an ENFJ, you are extremely loyal. Because of your warm and caring nature, you tend to make it your personal responsibility to make sure that the people you love are happy and safe. It is not unusual for you to place their needs above your own. This also applies to organizations and causes that you believe in. With that said, there is nothing you consider more unacceptable than betraying and hurting those you care about. Since loyalty is such a core aspect of who you are, you expect the people you love to be loyal to you as well. Being betrayed by someone you care about is one of the most painful things you can imagine.

6. Bringing Out the Best in Others

You believe in the potential of other people, and you want those people to realize it to the fullest. You genuinely want others to succeed. You gain immense personal satisfaction from knowing that you have contributed to another's success and well-being. Your positive energy is contagious, and you have a gift for making people come to life, and motivating and inspiring them to be the best they can possibly be. This quality is also connected to your natural gift for leadership.

7. Warmth and Sensitivity

You are sensitive to the concerns and emotions of other people. Because of your intuition, you are able to sense when something's bothering someone, even if they do not say it outright. You are sympathetic to their problems and will do everything in your power to help and support them. Your sensitivity also extends to the way you deal with people in general. You are able to reach out to others based on your understanding of their motivations and desires.

The 5 Greatest Areas of Improvement for an ENFJ

As an ENFJ, you are the carrier of many strong and remarkable qualities. However, there are also some areas of your personality that could use some improvement. These attributes are not limitations, but are simply natural inclinations of your personality type. It is important to understand that even though these are innate facets that make you who you are, you still hold the power to overcome them. Look at them as the first step toward achieving success and personal happiness.

1. Extreme Selflessness

A lot of your motivations as an ENFJ are rooted in your desire to help and support other people. While this allows you to contribute to the positive changes in their lives, it also causes you to become too invested. When you become too invested in someone you care about, you tend to take on their problems with the same intensity as though they were your own. This can result in bouts of self-doubt. Being too invested can also cause you to prioritize their needs before your own. It is important to understand that if you do not take care of your needs and well-being first, you will be unable to help them in the long run.

2. Shifting Self-Esteem

ENFJs are generally outgoing and confident. However, your self-esteem is not as stable as it seems to be. A perpetually see-sawing sense of worth is a common quality among ENFJs. This is caused by your idealism. You place great value on achieving goals and helping other people achieve theirs. If, for any reason, your goals and expectations are not met, your insecurity bubbles to the surface and you begin questioning your skills and abilities. This also happens when you are unable to help someone or when a person you are invested in fails to meet your expectations. Your self-esteem also takes a beating whenever there is conflict in your personal relationships. If you have just had a fight with a friend or loved one, you tend to replay the encounter in your head, trying to pinpoint what you did wrong. You often end up blaming yourself even when it is not your fault.

3. Having a Hard Time Saying No

You consider it your personal responsibility to make sure that the people around you feel happy, motivated, and valued. You are always willing to help however you can. In fact, people often turn to you for guidance and advice. Sometimes though, it can feel as though you are taking on too much. You cannot help everyone at the same time, but you find it seemingly impossible to turn them down. Furthermore, whenever you say no to someone, you end up feeling extremely guilty. You often feel like you have let them down or abandoned them. It is important for you to remember not to over-extend yourself; otherwise, you will become completely burned out.

4. Vulnerability to Perceived Conflict and Criticism

By nature, ENFJs are extremely sensitive. This is even more apparent during moments of conflict. In your daily life, you strive for harmonious relationships that are based on mutual trust. You consciously go out of your way to avoid conflict. When conflict becomes unavoidable, you tend to ignore the situation as an avoidance method. You would rather keep pretending that everything is okay than have to confront the negative situation head on. When it comes to criticism, it is hard for you not to see it as a personal attack. Because of your ideals, you tend to be very hard on yourself when you or your contributions are criticized. It is important for you to understand that criticism is meant as a constructive tool and should be seen from a purely objective standpoint.

5. Inflexibility

ENFJs act according to a strong sense of personal values. You feel strongly about your opinions. While you are generally tolerant and accepting of others' ideas and suggestions, there may be times when you can become inflexible in acknowledging beliefs that are different from your own. When this happens, you tend to shut out the new information and stick to what you know. When pushed, you can end up perceiving this as a personal attack which might lead to eventual conflict.

What Makes an ENFJ Happy?

An ENFJ is a "people-person." As such, you come alive when surrounded by other people. You feel comfortable and at ease whenever you find yourself in a large group. You enjoy building harmonious and deep personal relationships. The types of connections that make you happiest are those in which respect, appreciation, and loyalty are present. The bonds you share with others are of utmost importance to you. In fact, a large part of your personal happiness is based on the condition of your personal relationships.

You are driven by your loyalty to the people you care about, as well as to the causes and ideals that you believe in. Because of this, you are tireless in your efforts to extend assistance and support to those that need it. You have a bit of a superhero complex. You feel as though you are personally responsible for the happiness of others, and you take pride in seeing the people you love excel and succeed.

ENFJs are called Teachers for a reason. You enjoy being able to inspire and encourage people. You love helping them through motivation and support. You see it as a personal victory whenever someone you are invested in finally realizes their full potential and lives up to it. You have to be careful not to get too invested, though, because your sensitivity can cause you to take on their problems as if they were your own.

Because of your hypersensitivity to the feelings and emotions of others, the overall atmosphere of a situation can greatly affect you. As a result, you thrive in situations where the atmosphere is upbeat, encouraging, and generally positive. Conversely, you become exhausted when surrounded by negative energy, which is something you consciously avoid.

As an ENFJ, you require a sense of order. Without it, everything around you may seem chaotic. Due to this, you are happiest in settings where structure is prevalent. This is also evident in your personal life.

34

You go about your day with a clear schedule, and any deviation from that schedule makes you feel annoyed and uncomfortable. On the other hand, a happy and satisfying day for you would be one where all your plans were followed through. Furthermore, you find happiness in seeing your projects completed. There is nothing more satisfying for you than to see the results of all your hard work and planning.

What are Some Common Careers of an ENFJ?

Few decisions are as life changing as selecting a career path to pursue. Deciding on a career will have a strong and long-term impact on your life. As a result, careful consideration is recommended when making this decision.

It can be argued that anyone can become anything they want to be. That is true. However, certain careers are more in-sync with certain personality types. For example, an outgoing extrovert will not find satisfaction in a job that keeps them tied to a desk all day. Sure, they will be able to complete their tasks, but they might quickly burn out and exhaust themselves.

As an ENFJ, you are a natural leader with the ability to motivate and move people to action. You are a classic extrovert who thrives on harmonious social interactions, and you work best in environments with a clear set of guidelines and structural hierarchy. You are most likely to find satisfaction in careers that allow your natural strengths to flourish. Jobs that allow you to utilize your warmth, charisma, and communication skills are ideal. In contrast, careers that are too flexible do not appeal to you. You need to have a clear understanding of how your contributions are being assessed. You also dislike tasks that have to be completed just for the sake of completion. You have no problem with routine, but you prefer completing activities that will visibly benefit other people.

You possess the inimitable gift of being able to effectively persuade and convince people with your magnetism and flair with words. As a result, you are likely to fare well in jobs that involve persuasion, such as sales and marketing. Not only will you be able to do something you are good at, but the social aspects of those jobs are highly appealing to any ENFJ.

Another core aspect of an ENFJ's personality is the

drive to improve society and enrich people's lives. Because of this, it is highly likely that you will excel in the field of politics. As a natural born leader, this career path is the ultimate way to exercise your innate ability to lead. More than any other career, becoming a politician will give you the opportunity to motivate and inspire people on a much larger scale. Your language skills are also an invaluable asset in the political world. In fact, ENFJs are the most represented personality type among the presidents of the United States.

Your desire for structure and organization is another facet of your personality that comes into play when selecting a career. You enjoy planning and creating schedules, and it feels extremely satisfying when your plans are followed successfully. Organizing and facilitating events is an example of a career that will focus on those strengths. Becoming an event's organizer also appeals to your extroverted roots, because it allows building strong interpersonal relationships and be surrounded by other people.

ENFJs are also called Teachers, so it is no surprise that teaching is another career that suits the ENFJ personality. A career in education requires excellent organizational and interpersonal skills, both of which you possess in abundance. Being a teacher involves relating to other people while maintaining a structured environment, which is something that comes naturally to you. You are skilled at getting your message across to a diverse audience; hence you will have no problem reaching out to students with varying backgrounds. As a teacher, your ability to inspire and move people to action will be valued and appreciated. It also gives you the perfect avenue to help young minds develop and succeed.

As previously mentioned, ENFJs have the uncanny ability to adapt to other people's communication styles and overall demeanor. Because of this, people immediately feel comfortable and at ease around you. You also make it easier for others (even the shy ones) to open up to you. This quality makes you suited for jobs that involve building close relationships with other people, such as counseling, social work, and even psychology.

Overall, ENFJs thrive in structured work environments that foster close interactions with other people, while providing an avenue to motivate, encourage, and inspire.

Common Workplace Behaviors of an ENFJ

Whether you are a fresh graduate embarking on a new career or someone with years of experience under your belt, it is important to identify and understand the common behaviors you exhibit in the workplace. Understanding how you behave and how others perceive you can help you succeed.

In the workplace, ENFJs are driven toward being able to motivate other people. You are an enthusiastic and positive problem solver, and you utilize your ability to read people to foster a warm and supportive working environment. More often than not, you find yourself playing the role of a mentor, and you enjoy contributing to the success and development of those around you. As a result, you are drawn to positions of leadership. In fact, it is common for people to turn to you for assistance and guidance. You do not mind, of course. Your unique set of skills makes you perfect for that role. You are also an inspiring team player. You enjoy being part of a group, especially when working toward an altruistic goal.

Your contributions to the organization you work for are numerous and invaluable. Not only are you a catalyst that can push other people to action, you are also extremely loyal and reliable. When it comes to working environments, you flourish in settings that will allow you to interact with other people. Your ideal workplace is one with a clear, humanitarian mission that operates with a stable organizational hierarchy. You do your best work when you feel appreciated and valued by the people around you, so compliments and positive affirmations mean a lot to you in the workplace.

In positions of leadership, ENFJs are confident, inspiring, and action-focused. As a leader, you have a clear idea of what needs to be done to help the organization and its members. Regardless of the project at hand, ENFJ leaders remain undaunted and focused, all without losing sight of the team's condition and well-being. You use your sensitivity and communication skills to recognize the individual needs of your employees in order to build a stronger, more united team. As a result, your subordinates see you as someone to admire and emulate.

As a team member, ENFJs are cooperative and driven to succeed. You enjoy coming together with other people to work toward a common goal. Relationships are important to you, and it is no different in the workplace. You strive to create harmonious working relationships, and you use your intuition and sensitivity to do so. As an ENFJ, you are naturally enthusiastic, and often your enthusiasm can be quite contagious. It is easy for you to get people on board with your ideas and plans. However, your people-focused nature can also become a liability. Focusing too much on building meaningful relationships in the workplace might jeopardize the quality of the results you produce. Furthermore, becoming too invested and attached to the people you work with can cause you to lose sight of the objective nature of the job. When asked, your coworkers might describe you as helpful, friendly, and hardworking.

As an employee, you sometimes tend to underestimate your skills and abilities. In spite of that, you make quite an impression on your manager and colleagues. You are skilled at juggling multiple tasks at once without sacrificing the quality of your work. You are also a very fast learner. At work, your cheerful and enthusiastic nature shines through. You are always willing to help and take on new tasks. Your boss might describe you as reliable and efficient. However, less assertive ENFJs might find themselves being taken advantage of. Because of your willingness to help, you might agree to too many projects at once. Even though you know you are stretching yourself too thinly, your aversion to conflict and the desire to maintain a harmonious environment will keep you from saying no. It is important to understand that refusing is sometimes necessary to avoid exhausting yourself.

ENFJ: Parenting Style and Values

As an ENFJ, you are a sensitive and caring person who places great importance on personal relationships. In fact, one of the benchmarks of success for you is the overall condition of the relationships you have. You are a selfless giver, and you prioritize the needs of your loved ones more than your own.

The qualities that make ENFJs great leaders also make them great parents. As an ENFJ parent, you strive to find balance between being compassionate and caring, while instilling values and ideals. Overall, your parenting style is one that is based on encouragement and support.

Because you possess such advanced communication skills, you have no trouble expressing your affection through words and verbal affirmations. You also enjoy having long and meaningful conversations with your children. These encounters allow you to have a deep, emotional bond with them, which is something that parents with other personality types do not have with their children. You also utilize these one-on-one moments to impart wisdom and advice to help your kids. You are generous with praise and are quick to comfort them when they are feeling down.

You are a very hands-on parent. You take a very active role in your children's day-to-day lives. You schedule their activities, plan their meals, and make sure that everything is running smoothly. This is another way that you show them how much you care. Since you value relationships and connections, you also want your child to build meaningful friendships and have close family ties.

Boundaries and guidelines are important to you, but you want to make sure that your children adhere to them out of understanding, not just because you say so. For that reason, you try to encourage your children to explore and discover things on their own. That said, you consider it your personal mission to become a positive role model that your children can emulate, and you expect them to do so.

By nature, you are driven to nurture and care for the people you care about. This quality is emphasized even more when it comes to your children. You make it your primary goal to ensure their health and safety, and you strive for a home environment that is warm and free of conflict. As a result, you may sometimes find it difficult to enforce discipline and dole out punishments when your children misbehave. This is also connected to your discomfort with conflict and sensitivity to criticism.

As idealists, ENFJs can have very high expectations of other people. The same goes for your children. You assume that they will follow your example and lead a similar life to yours. However, as your children grow up, they will begin to make their own choices. There are times that those decisions might not be aligned with what you expect from them. This can cause you to feel hurt and undervalued. It is important to remember that this is just the natural process of raising a child, and that the values you taught them will always be a part of who they are.

Children raised by ENFJ parents grow up to be expressive and caring adults. They learn the importance of communication. They also learn how to build and maintain friendships and personal relationships.

Why Do ENFJs Make Good Friends?

Relationships are extremely important to ENFJs. For that reason, you are tireless in your efforts to keep friendships strong, regardless of distance and busy schedules. You actively find ways to stay close and connected to the people you care about.

You have no trouble meeting people and making new friends. You are confident and talkative, and you are not afraid to walk up to someone to introduce yourself. You are comfortable around strangers, and you have the ability to make strangers feel completely at ease around you. With you, strangers never stay strangers for very long.

ENFJs are the most people-oriented among the personality types. You are drawn to people, and people gravitate toward you as well. You also have the people skills to match. You possess a chameleon-like quality that allows you to bond with a diverse pool of individuals. Furthermore, you find genuine satisfaction in hearing their stories and getting to know them. You enjoy all sorts of conversations: average gossip, intellectual debates, and intimate talks. Even when opinions begin to clash, you find the mere back-and-forth of ideas utterly fascinating.

When asked, your friends are likely to describe you as fun, energetic, and supportive. You radiate with positive energy, and this makes you a joy to be around. Not only are you fun to hang out with, but you also make the effort to get to know your friends on a deeper and more intimate level. You are genuinely interested in their innermost thoughts and emotions, and you make them feel comfortable enough to open up to you.

Because of your intuition and sensitivity, you are able to gauge the shifts in the moods of your friends. You pay attention to the little things that indicate how they feel or how their day is going. If you notice that they are having a rough day, you are quick to cheer them up

51

and ask how you can help. If you notice that they are happy about something, you are there for them, armed with a celebratory smile.

As a friend, your loyalty is unparalleled, and so are the levels of your support and encouragement. It gives you great pleasure to see your friends succeeding and doing well in their endeavors. It gives you even greater pleasure when you've contributed to their success and well-being. You are always willing to help them in any way you can. If your friends have an idea for an interesting project, you are relentless in your efforts to push them forward. If one of them has a job interview coming up, you are the first to volunteer to ask practice questions. You are the kind of friend who rarely says no to someone in need. However, as mentioned previously, this is something you have to be careful about. If you are not careful, you may find yourself burned out and exhausted from taking on too much.

ENFJ Romance

As an ENFJ, you are a loyal and affectionate partner who brings out the best in your significant other.

For you, love involves finding someone who is honest, loyal, and affectionate. Your ideal mate is someone who values and appreciates you, and is not afraid to show it. These are the qualities you value most when looking for a partner. When you finally meet someone who fits that description, you tend to fall in love quickly and intensely. More than any other personality type, you throw caution to the wind when it comes to romance.

In terms of commitment, you seek out long term relationships that are based on mutual trust and respect. You are focused on the future. For that reason, you steer clear of casual encounters and random flings. You take your commitments seriously, and for you, being in a lasting relationship is the greatest and most important commitment of all. In fact, you feel safest and most at home when you are in a loving relationship.

As a lover, you place high importance on verbal communication. Even though your intuition can help you gauge your partner's overall temperament, you prefer talking about your emotions verbally. You consider it your personal mission to maintain a healthy relationship, and because of that, it is common for you to do an occasional "checkup" on the status of your relationship. This involves asking your partner about their emotions, issues, and concerns. Although you are coming from a place of genuine affection, this might be seen as being needy or even paranoid by partners with a different personality type.

In a relationship, it does not take much to make you happy. In fact, just knowing that your significant other is happy is enough to keep your heart warm. Making your mate happy is your primary goal, and you will do everything in your power to do just that. It is, however, important to you that your partner express that happiness through actions, words, and gestures of affirmation. You need to feel appreciated and valued, and when that does not happen, you feel neglected and unloved.

When it comes to intimacy, ENFJs are often skilled and affectionate lovers who are not hesitant about expressing their emotions. You view intimacy as a way of building an even stronger relationship.

Aside from that, you are an extremely supportive partner. You are always there to help your significant other achieve their goals, and you make it a point to inspire and motivate them. Their accomplishments make you proud, and you feel their joy as if it were your own.

Your aversion to conflict is particularly heightened in a relationship setting. You want your relationship to work smoothly, and you will do anything to keep things as peaceful as possible. During arguments or disagreements, you have the tendency to sweep things under the rug to avoid making things worse. However, your avoidant nature can sometimes be the very thing that might exacerbate the situation. It is important for you to understand that communication is key, and even the difficult conversations have to be had.

Best Personality Matches for ENFJs

Regardless of personality type, any two people can come together and have a healthy relationship, as long as there is trust and understanding. However, certain personality types just happen to fit well together. ENFJs are most compatible with INFP and INTP personalities.

The ENFJ-INTP and ENFJ-INFP combinations work well because an introverted lover will complement your extroverted nature. In return, you will be able to help your introverted partner come out of their shell. Being with a fellow intuitive is also ideal, because the two of you will have the shared capability to gauge each other's needs, emotions, and concerns. This is extremely important because intuitives have the tendency to forgo their own needs to take care of their partner's. Furthermore, the perceiving nature of INFPs and INTPs will help you loosen up a little.

Weaknesses

- Aversion to Conflict - You are extremely uncomfortable with conflict. For this reason, you avoid confrontations and arguments by sweeping things under the rug, so to speak. While this does temporarily prevent things from getting too heated, it is only a stopgap measure that can become unhealthy for your relationship. When ignored, important issues are not addressed which can lead to anger and resentment.

- Being Too Needy - Because you require appreciation and acknowledgment, you have the tendency to come across as needy and, sometimes, paranoid. You tend to hover over your partner at times, in an attempt to gauge the current status of your relationship. It is common for you to ask questions like, "What are you thinking?" or "How are you feeling?" Even though your intentions are noble, your partner might see this as being needy and worrisome.

- Your Chameleon-like Nature - You possess the chameleon-like ability to adapt to other people's behavior in order to relate to them. In most situations, this can be a valued strength. However, you have to be mindful not to carry this over into your romantic relationships. In your desire to be in a lasting relationship, you might mimic your partner's behaviors and interests, even though that is not who you really are. Sure, it might work for a while, but sooner or later, this will become exhausting for you.

Strengths

- Good Communication Skills - As a skilled communicator, you have no trouble expressing yourself. If you are happy, you make sure your partner feels appreciated and valued through actions and words of affirmation. If there is something that has been bothering you, you are able to get the message across as well.

- Encouragement and Support - You bring out the best in other people, especially your partner. You provide your partner with unconditional support and encouragement. You make them feel like they can do anything they set their mind to, and with your help, they probably can.

- Fun and Energetic - You are fun and energetic, making you a joy to be around. Your outgoing and energetic personality ensures that there is never a dull moment.

- Good at Planning and Budgeting - Because of the judging aspect of your personality, you enjoy living a structured and organized life. You have no trouble taking charge of the expenses, and you are quite skilled at budgeting and managing the cash flow. Furthermore, you are also an excellent planner, which ensures that both of your lives are running smoothly.

- Sensitivity and Warmth - You are naturally warm and sensitive. You are acutely aware of your partner's needs and emotions, and you make sure that all of those are being met.

7 Actionable Steps for Overcoming Your Weaknesses as an ENFJ

There is no paint-by-numbers approach to achieve success. That being said, understanding your weaknesses and knowing how to overcome them is an essential tool in personal development and self-actualization.

Here are a few actionable steps that you can do to overcome your weaknesses as an ENFJ.

1. Loosen Up

As an ENFJ with a strong affinity for judging, you can often come across as overbearing or controlling. To overcome this, try injecting a little spontaneity in your life. Start out with something small, like an impromptu trip to the movies or calling up a friend out of the blue to ask them out for lunch. By doing this, you will learn that last minute planning is not the end of the world. In fact, the most pleasant surprises can happen when you least expect them.

2. Embrace Solitude

As a card-carrying extrovert, the concept of being alone can be quite frightening to you. As an ENFJ, being alone causes your mind to work on overdrive, and you end up creating worst case scenarios in your head. Things can get dark really fast when this happens. For you, loneliness fosters self-doubt. This does not have to be the case. The next time you are alone, take the time to do something that makes you feel happy. It has to be something that does not involve talking to anyone else. Go out and get a massage. Stay at home and curl up with a good book and a mug of hot cocoa. Enjoy your own company. Understand that when you are alone, you are not really alone. You are with an exceptional human being: yourself.

3. See Yourself the Way Others Do

It has been established that you bring out other

people's full potential. You see the good in them, as well as their ability to succeed, and you do everything in your power to help them achieve that. However, when it comes to yourself, you can become quite critical. You often doubt your own strengths and capabilities. Without someone to remind you, you often forget just how wonderful you really are. Understand that you cannot always rely on others to make you feel good about yourself. Instead, learn to look at yourself as though you are looking at someone else. Notice all the qualities that make you shine. Focus on that. Repeat as needed.

4. Understand That No One is Perfect

You have high expectations of people, especially those you care about and feel invested in. So much, in fact, that it comes as a huge shock to you whenever they make mistakes that go against your idealization of them. Understand that, as human beings, they are likely to make a few mistakes. Understand that and accept them regardless.

5. Don't Exhaust Yourself

You are not Superman. You cannot take on everything all at once. Understandably, it is in your nature to want to help everyone with achieving their goals and solving their problems, but it is important to remember not to pile too much on your plate. It can end up draining and exhausting you completely. If you really want to continue helping other people, take care of yourself first.

6. Learn How to Say No

You find it hard to refuse when someone asks you for help, because you feel as though it is your personal mission to guide and support other people. However, you cannot fix everyone's problems. You cannot be there for everyone all the time. Learn how to say no once in a while without feeling guilty.

7. Realize That Conflict is Necessary

Your aversion to conflict can often prevent you from learning valuable life lessons. You dislike conflict so much that you go through great lengths just to avoid it. From pretending like nothing happened to giving up your own opinions just to appease others, you do everything in your power to keep the peace. However, it is important that you understand the significance of conflict. It is not always a bad thing. Oftentimes, it is just an indicator that an issue has to be addressed. Without acknowledging that there is a problem, it will only get worse. Sacrificing your own beliefs is not a healthy approach either. By keeping your thoughts to yourself, you are taking away learning opportunities from other people. Remember, some of the best solutions are born from conflict.

The 10 Most Influential ENFJs We Can Learn From

ENFJs are best known for their altruism, people skills, and natural ability to lead. When you put your unique qualities to good use, you can certainly accomplish remarkable things. Here are a few influential ENFJs who have inspired people all over the world with their gifts.

1. Martin Luther King, Jr.

Martin Luther King, Jr. was an American pastor, humanitarian, and activist. He is best known for his active role in the struggle against segregation, as well as for delivering the famous speech, *I Have a Dream*. True to his ENFJ nature, Martin Luther King, Jr. was a warm and compassionate leader with a gift for public speaking and the ability to move people to action.

2. Nelson Mandela

Nelson Mandela became the first black president of

South Africa after decades of activism against apartheid. He led the fight against organized racism and inequality after spending more than 20 years of his life imprisoned. He was never afraid to stand up for what he believed in, regardless of the consequence. He is the perfect example of a loyal ENFJ who would do anything for their cause.

3. Matthieu Ricard

Matthieu Ricard is a Buddhist monk who gave up his career in molecular genetics after he realized that science alone was not enough to give meaning to his life. Instead, he wanted to be able to inspire others to change their lives for the better. According to him, he does what he does to make other people more peaceful and emotionally balanced. He is the author of the book *Happiness*, which explores life's meaning and the fulfillment of being happy.

4. Oprah Winfrey

Oprah Winfrey is another ENFJ that has inspired and touched people all over the world. According to her, she is happiest when people are able to learn something from her and when she is able to enhance people's lives in ways they never thought possible.

5. Morgan Freeman

Morgan Freeman is an American actor and narrator who is best known for his deep and authoritative voice. He has received numerous awards for his outstanding acting performances. It is also important to note that Morgan Freeman often finds himself in roles of moral authority. In fact, he has portrayed God in two separate films.

6. Mikhail Gorbachev

Mikhail Gorbachev was the final leader of the Soviet Union before its collapse. He is best known for his hand in the collapse of the USSR and was awarded the

Nobel Peace Prize for his contributions. In an interview, Mikhail Gorbachev admitted that he had always possessed natural leadership skills. According to him, he was the friend that all his other friends turned to for advice and counsel.

7. Tony Blair

Tony Blair is a former UK prime minister who now focuses on charitable work. Tony Blair once admitted that he was highly intuitive when it comes to people's emotions, so he would sometimes use that ability to "manipulate" other people, for the greater good, of course.

8. Michael Moore

Michael Moore is an American director, writer, and producer whose films have moved and inspired people around the world. He is best known for his works such as Bowling for Columbine and Fahrenheit 9/11. He likes to use his films to spread awareness about important issues and possibly call people to action.

9. Bono

Bono is the front man of the rock band U2. He is also an activist and philanthropist. He fights against poverty, racism, and other issues our world is facing. He also uses his music to send clear messages of peace, harmony, and unity.

10. Reese Witherspoon

Reese Witherspoon is an American actress who has starred in a number of Hollywood films. According to her, she makes it a point to select roles that are pro-feminism.

Conclusion

ENFJs are extremely unique. Best described as inspiring and altruistic, you possess many special gifts that allow you to make a difference in other people's lives. Your kindness and sensitivity drive you to see the best in people and help them live up to their potential.

Your outgoing and friendly personality naturally draws people to you. Your intuition allows you to sense other people's needs and concerns so that you can address them. Your inclination toward feeling gives you compassion. Your preference for judging allows you to take on multiple tasks and projects without losing a sense of structure and organization. However, even your greatest strengths can work against you if you are not careful. Your desire to change people's lives can sometimes be seen as controlling and overbearing. Your sensitivity can sometimes foster thoughts of self-doubt. Your helpful nature can cause you to take on too much at once, making you neglect your own personal needs. Be that as it may, by applying the actionable steps mentioned earlier, you can overcome your weaknesses and be the best you can possibly be.

Selecting the right career path is extremely important, because it can be the avenue you need to exercise your unique gifts and abilities. Seek jobs that will utilize your people skills, while allowing you to implement change that will improve people's way of living. When it comes to friendships, surround yourself with people who appreciate and value you for your kindness and compassion. In terms of romantic relationships, never forget to take care of your own needs as well instead of solely focusing on the needs of your partner. Many ENFJs have used their gifts to ignite change in the world. You can do this too, if you set your mind to it.

Everything you have learned is meant to guide you in your journey toward success and self-actualization. Armed with a new sense of self-awareness, you can now face the world and all its challenges with a better understanding of yourself.

Final Word/About the Author

I was born and raised in Norwalk, Connecticut. Growing up, I could often be found spending afternoons reading in the local public library about management techniques and leadership styles, along with overall outlooks towards life. It was from spending those afternoons reading about how others have led productive lives that I was inspired to start studying patterns of human behavior and self-improvement. Usually I write works around sports to learn more about influential athletes in the hopes that from my writing, you the reader can walk away inspired to put in an equal if not greater amount of hard work and perseverance to pursue your goals. However, I began writing about psychology topics such as the Myers Brigg Type Indicator so that I could help others better understand why they act and think the way they do and how to build on their strengths while also identifying their weaknesses. If you enjoyed

ENFJ: Understanding & Relating with the Teacher please leave a review! Also, you can read more of my works on *ISFJs, ESFJs, How to be Witty, How to be Likeable, How to be Creative, Bargain Shopping, Productivity Hacks, Morning Meditation, Becoming a Father,* and *33 Life Lessons: Success Principles, Career Advice & Habits of Successful People* in the Kindle Store.

Like what you read?

If you love books on life, basketball, or productivity, check out my website at claytongeoffreys.com to join my exclusive list where I let you know about my latest books. Aside from being the first to hear about my latest releases, you can also download a free copy of *33 Life Lessons: Success Principles, Career Advice & Habits of Successful People.* See you there!

Made in the USA
Middletown, DE
23 July 2023

35625201R00046